RIGHT SIZING OUR LIVES

Hank Grimmer

PublishAmerica
Baltimore

© 2008 by Hank Grimmer.
All rights reserved. No part of this book may be reproduced, stored in a retrieval system or transmitted in any form or by any means without the prior written permission of the publishers, except by a reviewer who may quote brief passages in a review to be printed in a newspaper, magazine or journal.

First printing

PublishAmerica has allowed this work to remain exactly as the author intended, verbatim, without editorial input.

ISBN: 1-60474-568-1
PUBLISHED BY PUBLISHAMERICA, LLLP
www.publishamerica.com
Baltimore

Printed in the United States of America

ACKNOWLEDGEMENTS

I would like to thank the following people for their various types of support:

Scott Sherrill and Steve Dixon the developers and builders of SPICEWOOD, SPICEWOOD PARK, SPICEWOOD POND and SPICEWOOD at CEDAR RIDGE for their faith in me and their flexibility while I have been working on this project

Dr. Larry Wofford, owner of the Route 66 Harley-Davidson store, for his help in getting me started

Dr. Sandra Goodwin of the Bank of Oklahoma for her encouragement and technical assistance

And finally all of the people that I have come in contact with over the past five years who have been in the process of Right Sizing their lives

Foreword

The Author, Hank Grimmer, has captured every aspect of the "late in life" decisions necessary to make educated decisions regarding our lifestyle choices.

Covered in the book are the practical and the emotional choices of, not only the one who is in the golden years, but also to those responsible for and those in service to them.

Before moving mom or dad every adult child in the decision process should read this book. It is a complete handbook including the search for the "Right Size," moving from "my-home-for-ever," disposing of our no-longer-needed "treasures," and settling in with the new neighbors.

The author's empathy comes from his 30+ years of experience marketing homes to families of all ages and most recently to seniors.

Every family member, REALTOR, caretaker, and provider of services to the one entering the "Golden Years" should read this book carefully and provide it to your loved ones well in advance of the need.

Rodger Erker
1994 President
Oklahoma Association of Realtors
1996 Regional Vice-President
National Association of Realtors

Table of Contents

Introduction
…9
1. Motivations
…11
2. Emotions
…15
3. Location(s)
…19
4. Types of Residence
…22
5. Security
…26
6. Floor Plans
…29
7. Construction
…31
8. Gardening
…34
9. Exercise
…36
10. Nutrition
…39
11. Financing
…42
12. Stuff/Sorting
…50

13. Moving Companies
…53
14. Transportation
…55
15. Sale of Current Residence
…57
16. Now What
…61

Introduction

There are millions of people throughout the country who have reached the point in their lives that they feel that the time has come to make a household move. For many it is just a move within the same town or city. Others plan to move to a location which has been selected either because of their interests and hobbies or because their children and grand children live there. There are still others who will opt for two locations. However the location decision is made or whatever the motivation is, two things are common with everyone: *indecision and stress*.

The purpose of this writing is very simple. If we are able to reduce the level of *indecision*, we will also go a long way in eliminating *stress*.

Let us now go forth on the journey through the process we will all experience on our trip to our next home or homes.

HANK GRIMMER

NOTES

Chapter 1
Motivations

We should probably begin with determining what the motivation is for moving. There is not always just one reason for considering right-sizing your home.

I am going to present a list of possibilities from which may select as many as you wish or add as many as you wish.

- Being closer to my child/children and grand-child/children would be a good change
- My home is just too large
- My yard is just too much for me to take care of
- I would like to have a home with no stairs
- I would like to have something new, eliminating constant repairs
- I feel that I should be closer to medical facilities
- I would like to have a home that is accessible to people with physical limitations
- I would like to be able to lock the door and go away and know that I may stay away as long as I like and that my home

and yard will be in the same condition when I return that it was when I left
- It would be nice to be part of close-knit community of people my own age group
- I would like to live in a gated community
- Is it time to eliminate or distribute some things that have been accumulating over the years
- There is a need to continue the estate planning process
- The move should be made while I am still able to without depending on someone else doing it for me
- I would like to live in a home that my spouse can manage if something happens to me
- I am looking for a home that will appreciate in value

This list could go on and on, but I think that you have the general idea. Now let's examine some of these ideas in more detail to more clearly establish some of the criteria which will be important to you.

Probably the biggest motivation for people to relocate to a new city or state is the desire to have the ability to see their children and or grand children on a regular basis. Being able to visit with them on a monthly, weekly or even daily basis is a lot more enjoyable than seeing them at one or two holidays each year. It is not that we want to become more involved in their lives, but we do enjoy the opportunity to see them grow through the various stages of their careers and lives.

We also have to take into consideration that living in close proximity releases us from making long trips to visit. These trips seem to be over much too quickly, but we don't want to impose for long periods of time.

What we don't take into consideration is that by being closer, we also eliminate the feeling that our children have that they must make the annual or semi-annual trip to visit parents. Even though they enjoy visiting, it does take time and money that perhaps they would prefer spending on vacation or some other activities.

In combination with close proximity to family, perhaps the desire to adjust the size and style of our homes is the most frequent cause of people considering right-sizing their homes. Many of us decided years ago that because of the size of our families and our entertainment habits that we should have a two-story house. As we get a little older and the children have gone on we realize that we no longer need as many bedrooms and that we definitely don't need all those stairs. The obvious answer to that we consider a home that is all on one level and that perhaps life would be simpler if we adjusted the size. We will explore in depth the subject of new homes in Chapter 4.

In many cases our interests and hobbies have a great affect on our decision to "right-size" our lives. Many have avocations that we have dreamed of spending more time pursuing, and now we finally have the time.

Depending on the area of the country that we currently reside in, we have different reasons for perhaps relocating to follow our pleasures. For those who live in colder climates, the idea of moving to an area that affords us the opportunity to play golf year-round could be a good motivation. The same hold true for those who have a big love for the sport of fishing. Being able to go down to the waters edge on a daily basis or get in our boat and cruise and fish whenever we please is very appealing to many people. To those who are artistic, the ever-changing scenes of the mountains or the desert have a great appeal. The woods of some of our northern states hold some of the most beautiful lakes in the world and as a result are very appealing for those that want a place that has water, natural beauty and cool weather in the summer time. If our hobbies and interests can best be satisfied by a particular region of our country, location is a choice that we have to consider as we travel the road to right-sizing our lives and homes.

NOTES

Chapter 2
Emotions

At the end of Chapter One you found a blank page for you to make notes on. As we continue there will be a note page at the end of every chapter. It will be to your advantage to stop and think of the items that you feel you need to consider in that chapter and write them down on the note page. This will eliminate the extra burden of trying to remember all of the things in that chapter, and you will be able to go back and review the chapter just by reading your notes.

If you do this on a regular basis throughout the book you will not have the feeling of being overwhelmed by the process because you are taking control of the organization of your right-sizing process.

At this time my emotion is confusion. I am about to address the emotions of a couple, a woman or a man. In most cases the basic emotions are the same, but in the cases where people are alone the emotions are intensified.

There are so many things to consider that in many cases we do not know where to start. We are plagued with indecision. The most difficult thing to decide is: am I going to do anything? Deciding to act is the first step toward "Right Sizing" our lives. To make this decision we must deal with some fairly heavy emotions.

The first is that we are overwhelmed by all of the decisions that need to be made and all of the work that is involved. Perhaps the largest obstacle is that we do not know all of the choices or possibilities. We are going to try to eliminate this quandary through use of this guide.

The lack of knowledge concerning the process brings on the feelings of uncertainty and insecurity. For many this process is going to have to be completed without the aid of a spouse who had been involved in the decision making for many years. DO NOT FEEL THAT YOU ARE ALONE.

For those of you have children or grandchildren you may enlist their help in going through this wonderful experience of getting your life to a manageable state. Your children will help you with many of the selections and choices that have to be made. (After all, they have always thought they knew more than their parents). Another source of encouragement and help is friends who are in the same age group and have either gone through the process or are in the same boat that you are in. Having other people to visit with about the decisions seems to make it a lot simpler. If you have friends who have recently changed life styles to something that is appealing to you—-pick their brains.

One thing that is a great burden on those who are recently single is the feeling of loneliness. If this is one of the emotions that are driving your decision to change life styles, you should definitely consider moving closer to family members or into a community that is truly a community that affords you the opportunity interact on a regular basis with other people.

One of the results of involvement in all of this indecision and stress is that we may become depressed. The only comment that I am going to make concerning this is that the worst medicine for depression is solitude. If you are felling depressed at all—find someone to talk to about your feelings. Don't keep your feeling to yourself or decide to hide at home or bed until they go away.

We are going through whole process of "Right Sizing" to make our life more enjoyable, less stressful and more purposeful. Attack the whole process as a shopping trip that is going to fill your cart with relief and smiles.

What really are emotions other than the basis for our attitude? We have the ability as human beings to control our attitudes. We receive from others the mirror image of what we give to them. When you are positive, you elicit the same reactions from others. The sky is not going to fall so there is no need to act as if it were. When you look in a mirror, smile at yourself. It will either make you feel good or make you feel that you're a little crazy. People do not sing because they are happy, they sing to make themselves happy. If you can stand your own voice sing yourself a happy song, it will make you fell better. By the way, if you can't sing, but do watch T.V., watch something that is funny and uplifting. Even though we like to keep informed on a regular basis, there is no GOOD NEWS channel. What ever happened to people like Abbott and Costello, Lucy and Desi, Jack Benny and so many of the other funny people of a few years ago. Try to have an affect on someone else.

Let's make one decision right now. This is going to be a good experience and we are going to have a good time accomplishing our goal.

HANK GRIMMER

NOTES

Chapter 3
Locations

What we have been hearing all or our lives concerning the purchase of real estate are that the three most important things are location, location and location. This holds true now for our search for our new home, but the criteria has changed in determining what the most important things about the location are. We are no longer focused on locations that have the best school system and neighborhoods that have a lot of children or places that are convenient to extra curricular activities after school. What should we be considering?

During my conversations with over five thousand people in the process of "Right Sizing" there has been a fairly short list of what the most important considerations are.

The list is lead by the concern for proximity to medical facilities. Many of the people that I have visited with were in the process of moving from rural areas into an area that had hospitals and clinics that were going to be near their new homes. When you are considering the location into which you are going to move, keep this in mind.

Having shopping close is another of the things to consider when choosing a location. The two stores that seem to be the most important are grocery stores and pharmacies. These are the places that people visit on a regular basis and most folks do not want to travel a long distance to do their shopping.

Being within a couple of miles of a religious facility of the proper denomination is another thing to take into consideration. Churches are not only places of worship, but also centers of social activities. In many of the communities there is a "clubhouse" that becomes a social center, but if you live in a neighborhood that does not provide this the church provides the alternative.

Easy access to highways and the local airport is another thing to put in the equation. The majority of the people that we have dealt with are in a situation that allows that to travel at will. Whether it is by car or air, accessibility makes our lives less stressful. At the same time we do not want to locate in an area that has heavy traffic or a lot of traffic congestion.

The other consideration as far as location is concerned is associated with what our interests are: hobbies, sports, art, theater, golf, fishing and exercise. We want to be sure that we move into an area that has the facilities nearby to accommodate our needs as for recreation. Take the time to write down some of the things that are important from an entertainment standpoint.

NOTES

Chapter 4
Types of Residences

The first thing that we should take into consideration in this chapter is the number of residences. The reason for bringing this up is that we have visited with many people who have made the decision while they were "Right-Sizing" their lives that they should have multiple residences. The majority of the people we have talked with that have made the decision to have more than one residence did so from a climatic standpoint. Having residences in locations that have opposite climates affords us the opportunity to live in almost ideal weather on a year round basis. Whether you have decided to have multiple residences or a single location does not necessarily alter your decision as to the type of residence you choose.

The variety of types is limited and therefore we will take a look at each type.

The first and perhaps the most time consuming and complex is the single family home. The reason we say this is very simple: you have to maintain the entirety of the home and grounds. As you grow a little older some of you are finding that taking care of the yard, raking the leaves, planting the flower beds, and all of the other activities to properly maintain the grounds is becoming more difficult and less fun than it used to be. The solution to this problem is to hire someone else to do it for us, which of course is expensive. This being the case perhaps you should look at the next type of residence known as a patio home.

From an ownership standpoint patio homes are the same as owning a single-family home. You own the lot that the home is built on and the structure. From that point on living in a patio home is somewhat different than in a single family home. In most patio home communities all of the yard maintenance is included in your homeowner association fees. Most have central sprinkler systems, eliminating the need for you to water your yard. These two items by themselves give you the freedom to travel at any time and not have the worry of the upkeep of your property. Many patio home communities have a club- house that gives the residents a central gathering place for games, dinners, parties or just general socializing. Facilities of this type make transitioning to a new location much smoother in that you can instantly meet and become involved with people in your new community.

A community of town-houses can follow the same format as the patio home communities with the exception that most townhouses are two story dwellings. Most of the people that we have talked with feel that at this stage of their lives it is more sensible to opt for a one- story structure.

Condominium living is the next category that we should review. One of the big differences between condominiums and the other categories we have discussed is that you do not own the land or the structure. When you purchase a condominium you are actually purchasing the area of the structure from the interior walls in. You are also purchasing an undivided percentage of the property on which the project is built. The positive nature of this type of living is that all of maintenance is the responsibility of the condominium association, both yard and structure. In most cases condominiums are multi-story and closely compare to apartment living. Condominiums are generally built in very desirable locations and take advantage of the fact that they provide a large number of homes on a small piece of land.

The final entry in this category, before moving on to living that includes expanded services, is apartment living. This is fairly self-explanatory. You have no ownership, but have no responsibility for doing anything except paying the rent.

For some people this has been the answer to the question of where to move.

The other categories that you need to take into consideration are progressive health care living, assisted living, and nursing homes.

The concept behind progressive health care communities is that there is a "menu" of services that are available and you may add the service that fits your needs. You move into a unit that is basically an apartment. You are responsible for taking care of yourself with the exception that in many cases this type of facility will have a dinning room that you are able to have your meals in if you elect this option from the "menu." If your health situation changes and you are in need of care on a part-time basis you have the option of adding this item from the menu. Most of these types of facilities progress to the point of offering nursing home care. The advantage of these communities is that you are able to stay in the same facility and change health care environments.

I believe that you are aware of the assisted living and nursing home concepts so I am not going to address those options.

NOTES

Chapter 5
Security

We find that there are many items that contribute to an individuals feeling of security. These change from one person to another, but over all they make up a fairly short list.

From the standpoint of a community, perhaps that main amenity that people are looking for is what we all know as a "gated community." Gated communities vary slightly depending upon the construction, but generally they are completely enclosed in either a wall or fence system. As we would expect, the access to the community is controlled by a gate system. The majority of the gates are operated by a remote control that the individual may carry either on their person or in their automobile. By pointing the control at the gate and clicking, the gate opens. People who do not have a remote are unable to open the gates. Most of the gate systems have a box on the outside of the gate which enables a guest to telephone the resident to announce their arrival, and the resident has the ability of opening the gate by simply pressing a number on their telephone. Oh and by the way, if the caller is someone you don't want to see, you can always tell them that you are not home.

From the standpoint of the home itself, having a security system installed gives many people an additional feeling of security. We have observed that people who are living alone are more prone to having an alarm system installed. The majority of the alarm systems may be up-graded to include a panic button. This feature allows the owner to activate the alarm by merely pressing a button that may be carried with you. For people who are living alone or for those of us with health problems, there is a heightened feeling of security when this feature is included. The other electronic system that adds to the overall feeling of security is a smoke detector system. Knowing that you have an adequate number of smoke detectors in the home, gives us great peace of mind.

For those of us living in areas of the country that are affected by severe weather, there is another opportunity for us to add to our feeling of physical security. For many people the inclusion of a "safe room" in the residence is a very important item. These rooms may be included when the residence is built or may be added at a later date if the space is available. The specifications of these rooms vary with the needs of the individual.

Lastly and perhaps the most important "system" available is the community itself. If you live in a small community that is close knit, you have the greatest security of all. To know all of your neighbors and have the neighbors know you is the key to the feeling of "Total Security." When you live in a community that is made up primarily of people who are retired, you have the built in security of having your neighbors watching out for each other on a daily basis. Living in an area where this type of relationship will be established affords us all a very secure feeling.

HANK GRIMMER

NOTES

Chapter 6
Floor Plans

As we start our search for a new home another very important aspect of our search should be the floor plan that will best fit our needs at this time and in the future. I am going to list a few things that I feel are important items to take into consideration as we start looking at new homes.

- Is the home all on one level?
- Are the doorways and hallways wide enough to accommodate people with mobility limitations?
- Is the home completely without stairs?
- Does the home have an over abundance of windows?
- Are the ceilings at least nine feet high?
- Does the floor plan contain open/flowing spaces?
- Is the garage built in such a way that it will accommodate any type of vehicle, i.e. vans, suv's, pick up trucks, etc…?
- Are the bathrooms designed with extra open space?
- Is there adequate storage space?
- Is the utility room in a convenient location?
- Does the kitchen include all of the appliances I will need?

- Are the cabinets in the kitchen designed is such a way that they will be easy to access?
- Are there two bedrooms that each has its own bath?

These are a few of the things that we should look for as we go forward with our search. If you have special needs you should be sure that the homes that you are looking at meet your needs or can be modified to meet them. One of the things to keep in mind is that even though there may not be any special needs today, you should try to move into a home that will be comfortable for you under any circumstances in the future.

NOTES

Chapter 7
Construction

Now that we spent a few minutes giving consideration to floor plans, we should spend some time thinking about the manner in which our prospective new home should be constructed in order to meet our needs.

The first thing that we should look at is the materials that the exterior of the home is made with. One of the reasons that we want to start with this item is that the exterior of the home is the portion that in most cases requires the most maintenance. The most maintenance free construction is that which full masonry material. This category would include home which are built using stone, brick, Hardy Plank or any combination thereof. Rock and brick are self-explanatory. Hardi-Plank is material that is made of concrete and fiber: termites can't eat it, it will not burn, it is warranted for either 30 or 40 years, and it only needs to be painted every 12 to 15 years. One of the exterior construction materials to be leery of is synthetic stucco. In many parts of the country there have been major problems with houses constructed using this material when it has been improperly installed. We should also take into consideration the type of roof that is on the home, and the age of the roof. If we are considering a pre-owned home we want to make sure that the roof will not have to be replaced in the near future. We should also satisfy ourselves that the guttering on the house is sufficient to carry precipitation away from the structure and not allow it to stand next to the foundation or slab. Another item that we should consider in the thought process when thinking about the exterior of the home is the type of windows that have been installed. The windows are important not only from a light standpoint but also when considering the energy efficiency of the home. The most energy-efficient windows are those which are double pane glass with a thermal break that eliminates the conductivity of heat and cold into the home. Windows that tilt in for easy cleaning are another plus. You might want to consider looking for a home that is constructed in a way that there are no steps leading into the home. The size of the garage doors also is an area that we want to pay attention to. If the new home has garage doors that are ten feet wide it makes it much more convenient for parking vans, SUV's and large cars in the garage. You might also consider looking for homes that have ramps built in the garages that will accommodate vacuum cleaners, walkers, wheel chairs and perhaps your skateboard. Depending upon the area of the country that you live in, the amount of insulation that is used in the construction process is very important from an energy efficiency standpoint. Insulation with an "R" rating above r-15 is preferable. The higher the "R: rating the more energy efficient the dwelling becomes. Another consideration from an energy efficiency standpoint is the "SEER" rating of the air conditioning. With most manufacturers the warranty period is higher on units that are rated "13 seer" and above. The higher the rating the more energy efficient the unit is. You might also want to be sure that the home is wired for a security system, cable TV and telephone.

NOTES

CHAPTER 8
Gardening

You may be wondering why there is a chapter included in this book on gardening

The majority of the options for a new home that you are considering include the maintenance of the lawn, trimming. Edging and care of the shrubbery. If you decide on a new home that you actually own the dwelling and the land you will have the option of planting flowers and shrubs of your own choice.

You may be at an age that you no longer want the responsibility of caring for the grounds, but this does not eliminate the desire to surround yourself with the types of plants that make you feel good when you look at them. You also get a feeling of accomplishment knowing that you have planted and nourished the plants and flowers that you are looking at. You want to be very selective in the types things that you plant. The planting of perennials eliminates the need to put in new things each year. The planning of the type of flowers and plants should take into consideration the growing conditions most suited for the particular variety, i.e. full sun, no sun or partial sun.

We are in many cases going to be in a situation that we are no longer going to need our lawn mower, weed-eater, edger or hoses, but you want to be sure to keep the small tools that you use in the planting of decorative plants. By keeping them you will eliminate the necessity of going out and buying new ones at a later date.

There are very few that are as relaxing and self-satisfying than watching things grow that you have personally brought into the picture. In addition, spending time in your garden is a great use of time and wonderful therapy.

NOTES

CHAPTER 9
Exercise

To a lot of us exercise is/was a "bad" word. It was one of those things we never fit into our busy schedules. Now that we are retiring, exercise can easily become a part of a daily routine.

Keeping fit, maintaining our weight, and feeling energized are important priorities and can easily be accomplished in one's life. Staying fit provides the energy needed to maintain an active life of hobbies or even playing with the grandchildren.

Exercising can be done in a variety of ways depending on what you're trying to accomplish. There are two forms of exercise that can be done several times a week.

Walking is a great way to exercise. It can be done in the neighborhood, a local park, inside a mall or even on a machine at the local YMCA or health club.

Yoga, a beneficial, disciplined action means of exercise anyone can do irrespective of age, health or life circumstances. This can be done in your home by following a VCR or DVD tape; at a health club or the local YMCA.

- Walking is the easiest and safest exercise anyone can do.

- It easily fits into your schedule
- It is a way to delete fat and not muscle
- It burns calories and increases your metabolic levels
- It decreases your appetite
- Walking creates a sense of control over your body
- It slows the aging process
- It gets the muscles moving

Yoga is a means to create harmony within the body

- It brings the physical need for health, the psychological need of knowledge and the spiritual need of inner peace together
- It increases your body's flexibility
- It sharpens the intellect and aids concentration
- It brings awareness and the ability to be still and calms the mind.

So you say to yourself, "this is great, how can I get motivated to exercise?" There are several steps you can follow:

- Set a goal, a specific day and time to start your exercise plan. Keep it simple and realistic.
- Have a positive attitude so you keep and meet your exercise goals.
- You could start the day by listening to motivational tapes
- Read a chapter from a motivational or self-help book.
- Get an 'uplifting' theme song and listen to that in the morning
- Create some personal affirmations that you review daily.
- Keep a journal. Write down when you exercised and the foods you ate.
- Weigh yourself weekly or every two weeks, not daily. Keep this in your journal.

- Find a 'personal trainer' that you like and use them weekly to check your progress. The 'Y' or health clubs will have a source for you to check out.
- Walk, attend training sessions or Yoga classes with a buddy so you motivate each other.
- Visit your doctor and get a check up and let your doctor know what you plan to do if you are not use to exercising. Your doctor may have some suggestions or where to go or who to visit with so you meet your goals.

NOTES

Chapter 10
Nutrition

Everyone needs proper nutrition for the best possible physical health; productive work and play; and for a sense of well-being. It is number one in the battle against fatigue.

We have all noticed that as we age our body's food requirements change which means we need to be sure we are eating the foods that will be most valuable for our bodies. Adults and older people must be careful to avoid too many calories and still be sure to get enough nutrients and fiber to maintain food health.

Remember, we are what we eat so it is important to eat a variety of healthy foods every day. The number of servings you need from the five basic food groups will depend on your age, sex, size and how active you are. The food groups include: vegetables (3-5 servings daily); fruits (2-4 servings daily); milk, yogurt & cheese (2-3 servings daily); meat, poultry, fish, dry beans, eggs & nuts (2-3 servings daily); bread, cereal, rice & pasta (6 servings daily) fats, oils and sweets (use sparingly).

Today's high cost of living can make eating right a real challenge. Preparing your own meals gives you control over cost and nutrition. This reduces the need for "convenience" foods that are high in fat and contain preservatives. Preparing your own meals can be fun! How do you select nutritious foods?

Vegetables and Fruits:
- Buy them fresh.
- Buy frozen if what you desire is not available fresh.
- If you buy canned, check the labels for ingredients such as sugars and sodium.
- Breads, cereals, pastas and rice:
- Choose whole grain breads, cereals and pastas.
- Brown rice is better for you than white rice.
- Meat, poultry, fish, dry beans, eggs and nuts:
- Fish and poultry contain less fat and calories than red meat and are better for your health.
- Dry beans, peas or lentils are nutritious and a source of protein. Once cooked, they can be eaten as they are, mix them with cooked rice, or chill and place them in a salad.
- Red meat is harder for the system to process and contains fat and calories.

Buy nutritious snacks that are ready to eat:
- Carrots
- Celery
- Raisins
- Whole, unsalted nuts like almonds, filberts or Brazil nuts
- Peanut butter

Grow your own fresh vegetables and fruits:
- In the spring plant a garden, even if it is only a few items.
- Grow plants in containers if you do not have a yard.
- Extra produce can be frozen or canned for later use.

To find out more information about nutrition guidelines check with the following sources:
- Your health-care provided or family clinic.
- City or county health department.
- Local library.
- YMCA or Junior College for classes on nutrition or gardening.
- The dietitian at your local hospital.
- The local Arthritis or Diabetes Foundation for specific types of diets.

NOTES

Chapter 11
Financing

Bridge Loans

A "bridge loan" is financing that is secured by the equity and value of your current home. The proceeds from the loan are used to purchase your new home and the loan is repaid when your current home sells. A simple explanation is: a short term loan, with no up front fees and used to purchase your new home. This type of loan would normally be arranged by your personal banker. Another source of this type of financing is available if you have a large investment portfolio. If you have a large portfolio you have the option of borrowing the funds necessary to purchase your new home at a very low interest rate from your brokerage firm. Again, you would repay the loan at the time your present property is sold.

Mortgages
Conventional Financing

The conventional loan is a real estate loan that is not insured or guaranteed by any agency of the Federal Government.

The primary advantages associated with conventional financing are as follows:

1. Conventional loans usually require less time to process, approve, and close than FHA insured or VA guaranteed loans.

2. Conventional loans are available in amounts exceeding maximum loan amounts available under FHA or VA programs.

Conventional loans are available with as little as 5% of the purchase price as a down payment. However, conventional loans with less that 20% of the purchase price down are referred to as insured conventional loans and require private mortgage insurance or PMI.

Private Mortgage Insurance (PMI) us required is required on all conventional loans with less than 20% of the purchase price down and, in some cases, will be required when the down payment exceeds 20%. PMI is obtained from private sector companies such as the Mortgage Guaranty Insurance Corporation (MGIC) and General Electric Insurance Company. The cost of PMI will vary from company to company.

There is no maximum loan amount, as such, established for conventional loans as a general category. Rather, maximum loan amounts are established by each lender or investor such as The Federal National Mortgage Association (FNMA) or The Federal Home Loan Mortgage Corporation (FHLMC).

The current Single Family loan limit for both FNMA and FHLMC is $333,700.00. Loans that do not exceed this limit are referred to as Conforming Loans.

Conventional loans are available on an owner occupied or non-owner occupied basis. As a general rule non-owner loans require a *minimum* of 10% down and will, often times, require higher interest rates and/or fees than owner occupied loans. The interest rate on conventional loan is a matter of negotiation between the borrower and the lender. There are no controls, other than state usury laws, that in any way restrict conventional loan interest rates. The discount points required on a conventional loan are also a matter of negotiation between borrower and lender.

Reverse Mortgages

Things You Need to Know

What is a Reverse Mortgage?

A Reverse Mortgage is a special type of home loan that allows a homeowner to convert the equity in his or her home into cash. The equity built up over years of home mortgage payments can be paid to the homeowner: in a lump sum, in a stream of payments, or as a supplement to Social Security or other retirement funds. But unlike a traditional home equity loan or second mortgage, no repayment is required until the borrowers no longer use the home as their principal residence. HUD's Reverse Mortgage provides these benefits and it is federally-insured as well.

Can I qualify for a HUD Reverse Mortgage?

To be eligible for a HUD Reverse Mortgage, HUD's Federal Housing Administration requires that you are a homeowner 62 years old or older, have a very low outstanding mortgage balance or own your home free and clear, and that you meet with a HUD-approved counseling agency—-to make sure that you understand what a HUD Reverse Mortgage will mean to you.

Can I apply if I didn't buy my present home with FHAS mortgage insurance?

Yes. While your property must meet FHA minimum standards, it doesn't matter if you didn't buy it with an FHA-insured mortgage. Your new HUD Reverse Mortgage will be a new FHA-insured mortgage loan.

What if I own a condominium, not a single family home?

You can still qualify for HUD's Reverse Mortgage program. An eligible property must be your principal residence, but can be a single-family residence; a one-to four unit dwelling with one unit occupied by the borrower; a manufactured home (mobile home); a unit in FHA-approved condominiums; and planned unit developments. Your property must meet FH minimum property standards, but you can fund repairs from your Reverse Mortgage.

What is the difference between a Reverse Mortgage and a bank home equity loan?

With the traditional second mortgage, or home equity line of credit, you must have sufficient income to qualify for the loan, and you are required to make monthly mortgage payments. A Reverse Mortgage works very differently. The Reverse Mortgage pays you, and it is available regardless or your current income. You don't make payments, because the loan is not due as long as the house is your principal residence. Like all homeowners, you are still required to pay your real estate taxes and other conventional payments like utilities, but with and FHAS-insured HUD Reverse Mortgage, you cannot be foreclosed or forced to vacate your house because you "missed your mortgage payment."

Can the lender take my home away if I outlive the Loan?

NO! The loan does not become due until you home is sold, is no longer your primary residence or until you die. You cannot be forced to sell your home to pay off the mortgage loan even if the loan balance grows to exceed the value of the property. And, HUD's Federal Housing Administration guarantees that you'll receive all the payments that are owed you.

Will I still have an estate that I can leave to my heirs?

When you sell your house or no longer use it as your primary residence, you or your estate will repay the cash you received from the Reverse Mortgage, plus interest and other finance charges to the lender. All proceeds beyond what you owe belong to you or your estate. This means that the remaining equity in your home will be passed on to your heirs. None of your other assets will be affected by HUD's Reverse Mortgage loan. No debt will ever be passed along to the estate or heirs. You retain ownership or your home, and may sell or move at any time.

HOW REVERSE MORTGAGES WORK

Homeowners 62 and older who have paid off their mortgages or have only small mortgage balances remaining are eligible to participate in HUD's reverse mortgage program. The Program allows homeowners to borrow against the equity in their homes.

Homeowners can receive payments in a lump sum, on a monthly basis long (for a fixed term or as long as they live in the house), or on an occasional basis as a line of credit.

Homeowners whose circumstances change can restructure their payment options.

Unlike ordinary home equity loan, a HUD reverse mortgage does not require repayment as long as the borrower lives in the home. Lenders recover their principal, plus interest, when the home is sold or refinanced by the heirs. The remaining value of the home goes to the homeowner or to his or her survivors. If the sales proceeds are insufficient to the pay the amount owed, HUD will pay the lender the amount of the shortfall. The Federal Housing Administration, which is part of HUD, collects an insurance premium from all borrowers to provide this coverage.

The size of reverse mortgage loans is determined by the borrower's age, the interest rate, and the homes value. The older the borrower, the larger the percentage of the home value that can be borrowed.

For example, based on a loan at today's low interest rates, a 65 year-old could borrow 60 per cent of the home's value, a 75 year-old could borrow up to 70 per cent and an 85 year-old could borrow almost 80 per cent—up to the FHA loan limit for each city and county.

There are no asset or income limitations on borrowers receiving HUD's reverse mortgages.

There are also no limits on the value of homes qualifying for a HUD reverse mortgage, However, the amount that may be borrowed is capped by the maximum FHA loan limit for each city and county depending on the local housing cost.

HUD's reverse mortgage program collects funds from insurance premiums charged t borrowers. Senior citizens are charged 2 per cent of the home's value as an up-front payment plus one-half per cent of the loan balance each year. These amounts are usually paid by the lender and charged to the borrower's principal balance.

FHA's mortgage insurance guarantees to the borrowers that they will continue to receive their loan proceeds even if the Lender goes bankrupt. The FHA insurance also guarantees that they will get their money back with interest and fees even if the homeowners outlive the longevity tables or the property values decrease. Thus while the FHA mortgage insurance increases the initial cost of a HECM reverse mortgage, it also allows lenders to sell HCEM reverse mortgages at interest rates well below those of FannieMae and private lenders.

What Can You Do with the Money?

The proceeds from a reverse mortgage can be used for anything: daily living expenses; home repair or improvements; medical bills and prescription drugs; pay off of existing debts; education; travel; long- term health care; retirement and estate planning; and other needs you may have.

The proceeds from a reverse mortgage are available as a lump sum, fixed monthly payments for as long as you live in the property, a line of credit: or a combination of these options.

The amount of benefit that you will qualify for, will depend on your age at the time you apply for the loan, the type of reverse mortgage you choose, the value of your home, current interest rates, and for some products, where you live. As a general rule, the older you are and the greater your equity, the larger the reverse mortgage benefit will be.

The cost associated with getting a reverse mortgage are similar to those with a conventional mortgage, such as the origination fee, appraisal and inspection fees, title policy, mortgage insurance and other normal closing costs. With a reverse, all of these costs can be financed as part of the mortgage.

You must first meet with an independent reverse mortgage counselor before applying for a reverse mortgage. The counselor's job is to educate you about reverse mortgages, to inform you about your alternative options available to you given your situation, and assist you in determining which particular reverse mortgage product would best fit your needs if you elect to get a reverse mortgage. This counseling session is at no cost to the borrower and can be done in person or over the telephone.

NOTES

Chapter 12
Stuff/Sorting

No matter how long we have lived in a home we accumulate what I am going to refer to as "stuff." We have stuff in the attic, the closets, the garage, the basement, cabinets, storage buildings and just about any place else you can think of. What the heck are we going to do with all this "stuff"? Just about everything that we possess can be categorized under the general heading of "stuff."

One of our biggest challenges is to figure out what we will need and what there will be room for in our new home.

The place to start in this process of determining what we are going to being moving is with a floor plan of our new residence that is drawn to scale. The reason that we want to start here is that we now have a tool that will allow us to plan what furniture we will be able to use and where we will place it in the rooms. With a scaled plan you can then measure the furniture and cut out pieces of paper or "post-its" and place them on the floor plan. When doing this it is always helpful to know where there are electrical outlets, phone jacks and cable TV connections. The plan, because of the inclusion of closets and kitchen cabinet space, give you the sizes of what you are going to have for available storage space. One of the other things to consider is the amount of wall space in the garage that may be used after the installation of shelving. The final are to consider is any overhead storage space, whether it be over the garage or over the living areas. These areas are always handy for the storing of seasonal decorations, infrequently used items, etc.

Now that we have determined how much space is going to be available we can start the process of "sorting the stuff." I am going to suggest that as you go through this process that you start with items that have the most emotion attached to them, and as you determine that these are must keep items—-pack them in boxes and set them aside. If we eliminate most of the emotional stuff right up front it will make the rest of the process a lot less stressful. I will note at this time that these items should probably be the first things to be unpacked in your new residence in that they create the feeling of "the familiar" immediately.

You have now determined which furniture is definitely going to be used and what "stuff" will be in the closets, cabinets, on the kitchen counter, in the garage and in other storage space. Now we are then faced with the question: What do we do with the rest of this "stuff"??

The biggest consideration in determining what you are going to do with the excess is: what is going to be the least stressful way of disposing of this "stuff"?

The first alternative is our children or our grand-children. Since they have grown up with the "stuff" that we find that we will no longer be able to use there will definitely be items that they would like to have. This part of the process is fairly simple.

From this point there are a few alternatives. If you are dealing with a large quantity you may want to start by investigating either having an auction on site or having an auction company transfer your "stuff" to their facility. This process eliminates the necessity of you handling these items on a repetitive basis. They move it, sell and give you a check—minus their fees.

If you have a large amount of excess furniture you may want to consider company that operates a resale shop that would have merchandise of the same quality that you are trying to dispose of.

The next way to accomplish your task would be to hire a group that put on estate sales. Again, they do all of the work and you get the proceeds minus the fees.

From there we go the old standby....The Garage Sale. Oh what a hassle. Sorting, pricing, arranging, displaying and haggling. Then when it is all over you still have the unsold items to deal with.

It does not matter how you are able to complete this task, the important consideration is how to do it in the least stressful way. When I say stressful I am referring to both mental and physical stress. Keep in mind the whole move is going to be hard work for someone. Try to make it someone else.

NOTES

Chapter 13
Moving Companies

When the time arrives to make a decision on how to move you want to take care to select the company that best fits your needs.

If you are involved in a long move you will be better served by one of the many national moving companies. In most cases the fee for this type of moving is determined by the weight of the cargo. If is your situation you might want to make sure that you are not moving a lot of things which will not be needed in your new home.

If you are going to be involved in a local move you will want to look at local companies. In most cases they charge by the hour. There are some good ones and some that are not so great. Be sure to take the time to ask your friends who have recently moved what their experience has been and you should also consult with your real estate professional.

Depending on your budget and your age you should definitely consider have the moving company do all of the packing for you. You can supervise the packing so that is packed is such a way that the unpacking may be done by specific room, but you will feel better physically if you let someone else to all the hard work.

HANK GRIMMER

NOTES

Chapter 14
Transportation

There are just a few transportation items that you should take into consideration in the process of deciding the location for your new home.

The first and perhaps the most important on a daily basis is the ease of ingress and egress. You should be sure that you are not going to be in a situation that you are entering heavy traffic that will limit you ability to get into and out of you new community.

You also want to try to as close to an interstate as possible. If you are going to be traveling on a regular schedule it is much more convenient to have easy access to the highway system.

If you are going to be traveling by train or plane you should plan on being a convenient distance from the train station or the airport.

If you are going to be living in a large planned community it may be wise to consider investing in a golf cart for internal transportation.

The final consideration for those that are not able to or don't drive is a community that provides transportation for you. There are many places that provide shuttle service to shopping, health care facilities, churches, etc.

Transportation is not a huge issue, but it is something that you want to think about when deciding on your new location.

NOTES

Chapter 15
Sale of Current Residence

There are certain things that you want to accomplish in the process of selling your existing residence. You want to be able to get the best possible price, in the shortest period of time, under the best terms and conditions and with the least inconvenience to you.

To accomplish these goals there are basically only two ways to sell your house. The first is to sell it yourself and the second is to employ someone else to do it for you.

You should consider the steps in the selling process before making a decision on which option you are going to choose. The steps are as follows:

- Preparation of the property
- Pricing
- Marketing
- Showing
- Negotiations
- Contracts
- Inspections

- Renegotiation
- Closing

Every piece of property has two personalities. One is on the outside and the other on the inside. To present the total package to the prospective buyers you want to be sure that both areas are in the very best possible condition. The first thing that buyers see is the outside. You want to make the view from the curb as appealing as you possibly can. Having the lawn mowed, the shrubs trimmed and flowers planted are essential for a good first impression. The last item to consider is the front door. Be sure that your front door is inviting. Fresh paint is simple on the place that people will be waiting to enter the house. You know if there are any cosmetic improvements that need to be done to the interior. If you feel there are things that can be done easily that will enhance the picture of the interior take the time to have them done.

The only way to properly price your property is by using comparable data of houses that either on the market in area or that sold in the area.

Marketing is merely informing as many people as possible that your property is for sale as you possibly can. The most important item in the marketing strategy is the "For Sale" sign. Your neighbors will know that you are selling and tell their friends. People wanting to move into your area will see the sign. Everyone that drives by will see the sign and tell anyone who they know that your place is for sale. The sign is important, make sure it is a nice one.

Showing your property is another facet that you have to take into consideration when you are preparing to sell your residence. One big question is about safety. When someone rings your doorbell or calls to see your house you should be aware that there is no way of knowing why that person is calling. Ask as many questions as it takes to be comfortable with inviting a stranger in to see the property.

The rest of the items on the list are more complicated and a little more difficult to explain.

Negotiation directly between buyer and sell are very difficult because there is emotion involved. The seller won't necessarily tell the seller what they feel is wrong with the property because they don't want to hurt their feelings. The seller may not be firm enough with the prospective buyer because the do not want to jeopardize the possible sale. The end result may be that "nothing" happens at all.

Contracts vary from state to state. You will have to seek the advice of either and attorney or a real estate professional to learn what is applicable in your area.

All of the things that we have just reviewed can be handled easily if you decide to hire a REALTOR. Real estate is their profession. You pay a fee for the service that they provide, but we pay a fee to every professional that we engage whether is an accountant, a lawyer, a doctor or any other professional. Hiring someone to represent you will accomplish the four goals that you are trying to reach: the best possible price, in the shortest period of time, under the best terms and conditions and with the least inconvenience to you.

HANK GRIMMER

NOTES

Chapter 16
Now What

I have touched on the things I feel are the most important for you to consider while in the process of "Right-Sizing" your life.

There are many others you will encounter, but these are the most common.

Take your time in the planning process, be patient and have faith.